BISHOP JOHN'S LIST

The Entrepreneur's Blueprint

Cheat Sheet of Over 1400 Profitable Businesses in Africa and the Developing World

JOHN EGYAWAN

FORWARD

The continent of Africa is often viewed through a lens of its immense natural resources, rich cultures, and rapidly evolving economies. Yet, the true potential of Africa lies in its entrepreneurial spirit and the boundless opportunities that await those who dare to explore them. It is with great excitement and a sense of purpose that I present "The Bishop John's List - The Entrepreneur Blueprint: Cheat Sheet of Over 1400 Profitable Businesses in Africa and The Developing World."

Africa's narrative is shifting from a story of potential to one of realization. The dynamic economies, youthful populations, and increasing digital connectivity are paving the way for unprecedented growth. This book is more than just a list; it is a comprehensive guide to navigating the diverse and fertile business landscape of Africa.

I have witnessed firsthand the transformative power of entrepreneurship across this continent. From bustling cities to rural communities, innovation and resilience are driving economic empowerment and social progress. This book captures the essence of these opportunities, offering a roadmap for entrepreneurs, investors, and visionaries who are ready to contribute to Africa's growth story.

In compiling this guide, we have drawn from a wealth of sources, including industry reports, academic research, and direct insights from successful African business leaders. Our aim is to provide you with not only a list of potential ventures but also the knowledge and inspiration needed to turn these opportunities into thriving enterprises.

To the aspiring entrepreneur, I say this: Africa is calling. Whether you are starting a micro-business, entering a new industry, or looking to expand your investment portfolio, the potential for success is immense. This book is your starting point. It is designed to ignite your passion, inform your decisions, and guide your journey toward building a successful business in Africa.

Remember, the key to success is not just in recognizing opportunities but in taking bold steps to seize them. As you embark on this exciting journey, may you be inspired, motivated, and equipped to make a lasting impact on the vibrant tapestry of African entrepreneurship.

Welcome to the future of business in Africa. Welcome to "The Bishop John's List."

Sincerely,

John Egyawan

INTRODUCTION

The lists provided bellow are not exhaustive and may not be free from errors or omissions. The information provided is intended for general informational purposes only and should not be relied upon as business, financial, or legal advice. Before embarking on any business venture, it is important to conduct thorough research, seek professional guidance, and exercise due diligence to assess the feasibility and potential risks associated with any business endeavor.

Description of the Bishop John's List.

This list includes responses to various requests for profitable businesses across several industries in Africa. The lists are not exhaustive and are intended to provide a broad range of ideas and examples for entrepreneurs and investors seeking business opportunities in Africa. The lists contain 50 businesses for each industry or category requested, and care has been taken to avoid repetition wherever possible. It is important to note that the businesses listed are not guaranteed to be profitable, and individual research and analysis are necessary to assess the feasibility and profitability of any business venture. The information provided is intended for general informational purposes only and should not be considered a substitute for professional guidance or advice.

CONTENTS

	Forward	iv
	Introduction	vi
1	**Section A:**	Pg 1
	List of Profitable Industries to into in Africa	Pg 1
	List of 400 Profitable Micro Businesses in Africa	Pg 15
2	**Section B:**	Pg 26
	Agriculture Industry	Pg 26
	Mining Industry	Pg 32
	Real Estate Industry	Pg 26
	Telecommunication Industry	Pg 34
	Communication Industry	Pg 37
	Technology Industry	Pg 40
	Finance Industry	Pg 44
	Energy Industry	Pg 47
	Oil and Gas Industry	Pg 50
	Healthcare Industry	Pg 53
	Tourism Industry	Pg 55
	Fast-Moving Consumer Goods (FMCG) Industry	Pg 58
	Education Industry	Pg 60
	Transportation Industry	Pg 63
	Construction Industry	Pg 66
	Manufacturing Industry	Pg 68
	Service Industry	Pg 71
	Street Business (Buyam Sellem)	Pg 73
	Conclusion and disclaimer	Pg 77
	About the Author	Pg 80

SECTION A

LIST OF PROFITABLE INDUSTRIES TO INTO IN AFRICA.

1.   **Agriculture:**

Agriculture is the backbone of many african economies, with a large portion of the population engaged in farming. The continent has vast tracts of arable land and favorable climatic conditions that support the growth of various crops.

2.   **Mining:**

Africa is rich in mineral resources, with some of the largest deposits of gold, diamonds, and other precious metals and minerals found on the continent. Mining has traditionally been a significant contributor to many african economies.

3. **Real estate:**

The demand for real estate in Africa is on the rise, driven by a growing middle class and urbanization. There are opportunities for developers to build residential and commercial properties.

4. **Telecommunications:**

The telecommunications industry in Africa has been growing rapidly in recent years, driven by the increasing use of mobile phones and the internet.

5. **Financial services:**

There is a growing demand for financial services in Africa, with many people seeking to access banking and other financial products. The sector is also benefiting from the adoption of mobile banking and other innovative financial technologies.

6. **Energy:**

Africa has significant energy resources, including oil, gas, and renewable energy sources. There are opportunities for businesses involved in energy exploration, production, and distribution.

7. **Health care:**

The healthcare industry in Africa is growing as a result of population growth and increased demand for quality healthcare services. There is a need for private sector investment in this sector to support the growth of medical infrastructure, equipment, and technology.

8.   **Tourism:**

Africa is home to some of the most diverse and beautiful tourist attractions in the world, including natural wonders, wildlife, and cultural sites. There are many opportunities for entrepreneurs to invest in tourism infrastructure and services, such as hotels, resorts, and travel agencies.

9.   **Fast-Moving Consumer Goods (FMCG):**

FMCG is a high-growth sector in Africa, driven by a young and growing population and rising consumer demand for goods and services. There are opportunities for businesses involved in manufacturing, distribution, and retail of fast-moving consumer goods such as food, beverages, and household items.

10.   **Education**:

The education sector in Africa is rapidly growing, with a high demand for quality education services. There are opportunities for businesses involved in building and managing schools and universities, as well as those providing educational materials and technologies.

11.   **Transportation:**

Transportation is a critical infrastructure sector in Africa, with growing demand for efficient and reliable transport services. There are opportunities for businesses involved in road, rail, air, and sea transportation, as well as those providing logistics and supply chain services.

12. **Construction:**

The construction industry in Africa is rapidly growing, driven by urbanization and infrastructure development. There are opportunities for businesses involved in building and managing infrastructure such as roads, bridges, housing, and commercial buildings.

Overall, Africa presents many opportunities for businesses across a range of industries. However, it is essential to do thorough research and due diligence before investing in any sector or market on the continent, as there are also significant risks and challenges to consider.

List of 400 profitable micro business that can be done in Africa also applicable in most of the developing nations.

Here are some examples of micro businesses that have the potential to be successful in Africa:

Before proceeding to the list i would like you to take note of the following:

1.   Starting a micro business can be a rewarding and fulfilling experience, but it requires hard work, dedication, and a willingness to learn and adapt to new challenges. It's important to have a clear understanding of your business goals, target market, and competition before you start, and to continually assess your progress and make changes as needed to ensure success.

2.   When starting a micro business, it's important to have a clear understanding of the regulations and requirements in your area, including licensing, taxes, and insurance. You should also consider seeking advice from legal and financial experts to help you navigate the various challenges that may arise as your business grows and evolves. Good luck with your new venture!

3.   Starting a micro business can be a challenging and rewarding experience, but it takes time, effort, and dedication to succeed. Be sure to do your research, create a solid business plan, and continuously evaluate your progress to make any necessary changes and adaptations along the way. With hard work and determination, you can turn your small business into a thriving and profitable enterprise!

4.   When starting a micro business, it's important to choose a business that you are passionate about and knowledgeable in, so you can effectively meet the needs and demands of your target market. Be sure to invest in marketing and advertising to reach a wider audience, and continuously work to improve your products, services, and customer satisfaction. With a solid foundation and a commitment to excellence, your micro business can achieve great success and long-term profitability!

5.   It's important to continually evaluate and improve your micro business in order to remain competitive and meet the ever-changing demands of your target market. This can involve expanding your offerings, improving customer service, and exploring new and innovative ways to reach your audience. With hard work and determination, you can grow your micro business into a successful and profitable enterprise!

A LIST OF 400 PROFITABLE BUSINESSES IN AFRICA FROM VARIOUS INDUSTRIES

400 PROFITABLE BUSINESSES IN AFRICA FROM VARIOUS INDUSTRIES

1. Agro-processing (e.g., cassava flour production)

2. Baked goods (e.g., bread, pastries)

3. Beauty and personal care (e.g., hair braiding, nail salon)

4. Bicycle repair and maintenance

5. Catering services

6. Charcoal production and sales

7. Cleaning and laundry services

8.   Computer repair and maintenance

9.   Construction services (e.g., bricklaying, carpentry)

10.   Cosmetics production and sales

11.   Crafts and handmade goods (e.g., beadwork, pottery)

12.   Dairy farming and milk processing

13.   Electrical repair and maintenance

14.   Event planning and coordination

15.   Fashion design and tailoring

16.   Food vending (e.g., street food)

17.   Fruit and vegetable farming and sales

18.   Furniture production and sales

19.   Garden maintenance and landscaping

20.   Hair salon services

21.   Home appliance repair and maintenance

22.   Home tutoring and childcare services

23.   Horticulture and floriculture

24.   Ice production and sales

25.   Import and export services

26.   Information technology services (e.g., web design, computer programming)

27.   Jewelry design and production

28.   Kitchen and bath design and remodeling

29.   Livestock farming (e.g., chicken, goat)

30. Mobile phone repair and maintenance

31. Music and dance instruction

32. Organic food production and sales

33. Painting and wallpapering services

34. Pest control services

35. Pet care services (e.g., pet grooming, pet sitting)

36. Photography and videography services

37. Printing services (e.g., brochures, business cards)

38. Professional organizing and decluttering services

39. Real estate services (e.g., property management, rental services)

40. Recycling services

41. Restaurant and food services

42. Sales of second-hand goods (e.g., clothing, electronics)

43. Seafood processing and sales

44. Seed production and sales

45. Sewing and alterations services

46. Soap and detergent production

47. Solar panel installation and maintenance

48. Tailoring and clothing design

49. Technology training and consulting services

50. Translation and interpretation services

51. Transport services (e.g., taxi, delivery services)

52. Travel agency services

53. Tutoring and coaching services (e.g., academic, athletic)

54. Upholstery and furniture repair services

55. Vehicle rental services

56. Video production and editing services

57. Web hosting and online storage services

58. Welding and metal fabrication services

59. Wine and spirits production and sales

60. Woodworking and carpentry services

61. Yoga and fitness instruction

62. Youth services (e.g., after-school programs, summer camps)

63. Agricultural waste management and composting

64. Alternative energy consulting and installation services

65. Artisanal food production (e.g., cheese, honey)

66. Audio and video equipment rental services

67. Baking and confectionery production

68. Barber and beauty supplies retail

69. Bicycle rental and tour services

70. Bookkeeping and accounting services

71. Building inspection and assessment services

72. Call center services

73. Car washing and detailing services

74.   Carpentry and cabinetry services

75.   Cell phone and accessories retail

76.   Children's toy and game production and sales

77.   Clean energy consulting and installation services

78.   Clothing and textile design and production

79.   Coffee and tea production and sales

80.   Community development and outreach services

81.   Construction and demolition waste management

82.   Cooking and baking classes and instruction

83.   Corporate training and development services

84.   Custom signage and graphics production

85.   Delivery and courier services

86.   Digital marketing and advertising services

87.   E-commerce and online retail services

88.   Educational toy and game production and sales

89.   Electric vehicle charging station installation and maintenance

90.   Energy efficiency consulting and installation services

91.   Environmental consulting and management services

92.   Ethical clothing and textile production and sales

93.   Event and party rental services

94.   Event ticketing and promotion services

95.   Executive and personal coaching services

96. Fabric and textile retail

97. Fashion and accessories retail

98. Film and video production services

99. Financial planning and investment services

100. Fire protection and safety services

101. Fish farming and aquaculture

102. Floral design and arrangements

103. Food packaging and labeling services

104. Food truck and mobile catering services

105. Funeral and cremation services

106. Garden design and landscaping services

107. Gift basket and hamper production and sales

108. Glass and window repair and replacement services

109. Graphic and logo design services

110. Health and wellness services (e.g., massage, acupuncture)

111. Home cleaning and organization services

112. Home decor and furniture retail

113. Home energy audit and retrofit services

114. Horse riding lessons and trail rides

115. Hotel and accommodation booking services

116. Human resources and payroll services

117. Hunting and fishing guide services

118. Import and export brokerage services

119. Indoor and outdoor plant care services

120. Industrial cleaning and maintenance services

121. Information security and data protection services

122. Interior design and decorating services

123. IT support and network administration services

124. Jewelry and watch repair services

125. Kitchen and bath remodeling services

126. Language and cultural exchange services

127. Leather goods production and sales

128. Legal document preparation and filing services

129. Lifestyle and wellness coaching services

130. Limousine and private car services

131. Lingerie and intimate apparel production and sales

132. Locksmith and security services

133. Logistics and supply chain management services

134. Maid and housekeeping services

135. Marketing research and analysis services

136. Medical equipment and supplies retail

137. Medical billing and coding services

138. Medical equipment repair and maintenance services

139. Medical transcription and document management services

140.   Men's grooming and barber services

141.   Mobile app development services

142.   Moving and storage services

143.   Music and entertainment booking services

144.   Music composition and production services

145.   Natural beauty and personal care product production and sales

146.   Nature and wildlife tour services

147.   Office and business supplies retail

148.   Online marketplace services

149.   Online tutoring and education services

150.   Organic farming and gardening services

151.   Outdoor gear and equipment retail

152.   Pest control services

153.   Pet grooming and boarding services

154.   Pet sitting and dog walking services

155.   Pharmacy and medical supplies retail

156.   Photography and videography services

157.   Physical therapy and rehabilitation services

158.   Plant nursery and garden center services

159.   Plumbing and heating services

160.   Political consulting and campaign management services

161.   Pool and spa maintenance and cleaning services

162. Printing and publishing services

163. Private investigation and security services

164. Professional development and training services

165. Property management and maintenance services

166. Psychicotherapy and counseling services

167. Public relations and media services

168. Real estate appraisal and assessment services

169. Real estate brokerage and investment services

170. Recycling and waste management services

171. Refrigeration and HVAC services

172. Restaurant and food service management services

173. Retail and wholesale distribution services

174. Sales and marketing consulting services

175. School and daycare transportation services

176. Screen printing and embroidery services

177. Search engine optimization and digital marketing services

178. Security and surveillance services

179. Senior care and home health services

180. Social media management and marketing services

181. Solar panel installation and maintenance services

182. Spa and wellness center services

183. Sport and recreation event management services

184. Sports equipment retail and rental services

185. Steel fabrication and welding services

186. Storage and organization services

187. Stress management and life coaching services

188. Structural engineering and design services

189. Substance abuse treatment and rehabilitation services

190. Sustainability consulting and green building services

191. Tailoring and alterations services

192. Tax preparation and accounting services

193. Technology and gadget repair services

194. Telecommunication and networking services

195. Translation and interpretation services

196. Transportation and logistics services

197. Travel and tourism services

198. Tree trimming and removal services

199. Tutoring and education services

200. Urban farming and gardening services

201. Vehicle maintenance and repair services

202. Video game design and development services

203. Video production and post-production services

204. Virtual event planning and production services

205. Virtual interior design and decorating services

206. Virtual personal shopping and styling services

207. Virtual tour services

208. Web design and development services

209. Wedding and event planning services

210. Welding and metal fabrication services

211. Wellness and fitness coaching services

212. Window cleaning and pressure washing services

213. Wine and liquor retail and distribution services

214. Woodworking and carpentry services

215. Writing and editing services

216. Yoga and Pilates instruction services

217. Youth sports and fitness programs

218. Zoo and wildlife park management services

219. Agricultural production and sales

220. Art and craft retail and distribution

221. Audio and video equipment rental services

222. Auto detailing and cleaning services

223. Baked goods production and sales

224. Barber and hair salon services

225. Bicycle repair and maintenance services

226. Bookkeeping and accounting services

227. Building and construction services

228. Business consulting and coaching services

229. Car rental and leasing services

230. Catering and event planning services

231. Cell phone repair and unlocking services

232. Child care and nanny services

233. Clothing and accessory production and sales

234. Community and social services

235. Computer repair and IT services

236. Cooking and baking classes and services

237. Cosmetics and beauty product production and sales

238. Costume and prop rental services

239. Craft brewing and distillation services

240. Custom jewelry and watch production services

241. Dance and performing arts instruction services

242. Data analysis and management services

243. Dental equipment and supplies retail

244. Dental lab and prosthodontic services

245. Digital marketing and advertising services

246. Dog walking and pet sitting services

247. Dry cleaning and laundry services

248. Education and tutoring services

249. Electric vehicle charging and maintenance services

250. Emergency preparedness and response services

251. Employment solutions and market research

252. Employment solutions and market research

253. Estate planning and probate services

254. Event management and planning services

255. Event photography and videography services

256. Expediting and courier services

257. Financial planning and investment services

258. Fire and water damage restoration services

259. Fish and aquarium sales and maintenance services

260. Fitness and personal training services

261. Flood and water damage repair services

262. Food and beverage production and distribution services

263. Footwear production and retail services

264. Foreign language instruction services

265. Formal wear rental and sales services

266. Fragrance production and sales services

267. Freight forwarding and logistics services

268. Funeral and memorial services

269. Furniture and home décor production and sales services

270. Garden and landscape design services

271. Gift basket and floral arrangement services

272. Glass and mirror fabrication and installation services

273. Golf course management and maintenance services

274. Government procurement and contract management services

275. Graphic design and branding services

276. Green energy consulting and installation services

277. Handyman and repair services

278. Health and wellness coaching services

279. Health food production and retail services

280. Heating and cooling services

281. Heavy equipment rental and maintenance services

282. High-end luxury goods production and sales services

283. Home cleaning and organizing services

284. Home health care services

285. Home security and surveillance services

286. Horse and stable management services

287. Hospitality and tourism services

288. House painting and wallpapering services

289. Human resources consulting and management services

290. Hunting and fishing guide services

291. Import and export services

292. Industrial design and product development services

293. Information technology and cybersecurity services

294. Interior design and renovation services

295. Internet of Things (IoT) consulting services

296. Inventory management and supply chain services

297. Investment management and financial planning services

298. Irrigation and water management services

299. IT and computer support services

300. Jewelry production and retail services

301. Kitchen and bath remodeling services

302. Language translation and interpretation services

303. Lawn care and landscaping services

304. Leather goods production and retail services

305. LED lighting and energy solutions services

306. Legal services and consultation

307. Lifestyle and personal development coaching services

308. Limousine and transportation services

309. Lingerie and intimate apparel production and retail services

310. Locksmith and security services

311. Logistics and supply chain management services

312. Luggage and leather goods production and retail services

313. Maid and cleaning services

314. Makeup and beauty services

315. Management consulting and advisory services

316. Manufacturing and production services

317. Marketing and advertising services

318. Massage therapy and spa services

319. Meat and poultry production and sales

320. Medical billing and coding services

321. Medical equipment and supplies retail services

322. Medical lab and diagnostic services

323. Medical staffing and recruitment services

324. Medical transcription and documentation services

325. Mental health and wellness services

326. Merchant services and payment processing

327. Metal fabrication and welding services

328. Mobile app development services

329. Modeling and talent agency services

330. Mortgage brokerage and loan services

331. Motorcycle repair and maintenance services

332. Music and entertainment services

333. Nail salon and spa services

334. Natural and organic food production and retail services

335. Network and infrastructure consulting services

336. Nonprofit management and consulting services

337. Office cleaning and maintenance services

338. Office equipment and supplies retail services

339. Office furniture and space planning services

340. Online marketplace and e-commerce services

341. Online tutoring and education services

342. Outdoor adventure and travel services

343. Packaging and shipping services

344. Painting and wallpaper services

345. Party and event rental services

346. Payroll and employee benefits services

347. Personal assistant and concierge services

348. Personal shopping and styling services

349. Pest control and extermination services

350. Pet grooming and boarding services

351. Pet sitting and dog walking services

352. Pet supplies and accessories production and retail services

353. Pharmacy and medical supply services

354. Photography and videography services

355. Physical therapy and rehabilitation services

356. Plumbing and heating services

357. Pool cleaning and maintenance services

358. Power washing and exterior cleaning services

359. Printing and custom graphics services

360. Private investigation and security services

361. Product design and development services

362. Professional organization and decluttering services

363. Property management and leasing services

364. Public relations and media services

365. Quality control and inspection services

366. Real estate appraisal and valuation services

367. Real estate brokerage and consulting services

368. Recruitment and staffing services

369. Renewable energy consulting and installation services

370. Research and development services

371. Residential and commercial cleaning services

372. Restaurant and food service consulting services

373. Retail sales and product demonstrations services

374. Risk management and insurance services

375. Roofing and exterior repair services

376. Sales and marketing consulting services

377. Salon and hair care services

378. Sandwich and deli production and retail services

379. Satellite and cable installation services

380. School and educational support services

381. Scientific research and development services

382. Screen printing and custom apparel services

383. Search engine optimization (SEO) and marketing services

384. Security and surveillance services

385. Senior care and support services

386. SEO and digital marketing services

387. Service and repair of electronic devices

388. Share economy and peer-to-peer services

389. Shipping and logistics services

390. Shoes and footwear production and retail services

391. Signage and graphics production services

392. Skin care and beauty treatment services

393. Sleep diagnosis and treatment services

394. Small engine repair and maintenance services

395. Social media management and marketing services

396. Software development and IT services

397. Solar energy consulting and installation services

398. Spa and wellness services

399. Specialty food production and retail services

400. Sports and fitness coaching and training services.

SECTION B

INDUSTRY-SPECIFIC PROFITABLE BUSINESSES

1. AGRICULTURE INDUSTRY

1. Crop production and farming
2. Livestock production and farming
3. Greenhouse and hydroponic agriculture
4. Aquaculture and fish farming
5. Organic agriculture and food production
6. Irrigation systems and equipment
7. Agriculture machinery and equipment sales and repair
8. Agricultural waste management and composting services
9. Agriculture consulting and advisory services
10. Agricultural tourism and agritainment services
11. Agricultural financing and insurance services

12. Agricultural education and training services

13. Agricultural research and development services

14. Agricultural product processing and packaging services

15. Agricultural product distribution and wholesaling services

16. Agricultural product export and import services

17. Agricultural product marketing and advertising services

18. Agricultural product storage and warehousing services

19. Agricultural product retail and sales services

20. Agricultural land management and leasing services

21. Agricultural insurance and risk management services

22. Agricultural technology and data management services

23. Agricultural transportation and logistics services

24. Agricultural product inspection and quality control services

25. Agricultural energy solutions and renewable energy services

26. Agricultural water management and conservation services

27. Agricultural product traceability and certification services

28. Agricultural product labeling and branding services

29. Agricultural product certification and licensing services

30. Agricultural product safety and regulatory compliance services

31. Agricultural product price analysis and market research services

32. Agricultural product demonstration and field trial services

33. Agricultural product labeling and packaging design services

34. Agricultural product sustainability and environmentally friendly services

35. Agricultural product testing and analysis services

36. Agricultural product traceability and provenance services

37. Agricultural product promotion and public relations services

38. Agricultural product innovation and product development services

39. Agricultural product marketing and consumer research services

40. Agricultural product market analysis and strategy services

41. Agricultural product advertising and media services

42. Agricultural product branding and reputation

management services

43. Agricultural product brand management and licensing services

44. Agricultural product marketing research and data analysis services

45. Agricultural product pricing strategy and market analysis services

46. Agricultural product distribution channel management services

47. Agricultural product sales channel optimization services

48. Agricultural product sales and marketing training services

49. Agricultural product sales and business development services

50. Agricultural product supply chain management and optimization services

2. MINING INDUSTRY

1. Mineral exploration and geology services
2. Diamond and precious stone mining
3. Gold and precious metal mining
4. Copper, nickel and other base metal mining

5. Iron ore and steel production

6. Coal and energy resource mining

7. Uranium and nuclear fuel production

8. Mineral processing and refining services

9. Mining equipment and machinery sales and maintenance services

10. Mining transportation and logistics services

11. Mining waste management and reclamation services

12. Mining engineering and consulting services

13. Mining safety and regulatory compliance services

14. Mining financial and investment services

15. Mining insurance and risk management services

16. Mining land and resource management services

17. Mining technology and automation services

18. Mining research and development services

19. Mining education and training services

20. Mining water management and conservation services

21. Mining environmental management and sustainability services

22. Mining labor and human resources management services

23. Mining marketing and sales services

24. Mining marketing research and consumer analysis

services

25. Mining market analysis and strategy services

26. Mining supply chain management and optimization services

27. Mining product processing and packaging services

28. Mining product distribution and wholesaling services

29. Mining product export and import services

30. Mining product branding and reputation management services

31. Mining product certification and licensing services

32. Mining product traceability and provenance services

33. Mining product innovation and product development services

34. Mining product marketing and advertising services

35. Mining product market analysis and strategy services

36. Mining product pricing strategy and market analysis services

37. Mining product distribution channel management services

38. Mining product sales channel optimization services

39. Mining product sales and marketing training services

40. Mining product sales and business development services

41. Mining product supply chain management and optimization services

42. Mining investment and financial services

43. Mining security and surveillance services

44. Mining labor and employment services

45. Mining equipment leasing and financing services

46. Mining product labeling and packaging design services

47. Mining product sustainability and environmentally friendly services

48. Mining product safety and regulatory compliance services

49. Mining product testing and analysis services

50. Mining product traceability and certification services

3. REAL ESTATE INDUSTRY

1. Real estate crowdfunding platforms

2. Property staging and interior design

3. Property listing and search websites

4. Property auctioneering services

5. Vacation rental management services

6. Property management training and education

7. Real estate litigation and dispute resolution

8. Property management franchise opportunities

9. Real estate advertising and marketing agencies

10. Real estate law firms and legal services

11. Real estate investment seminars and workshops

12. Real estate equity and debt financing

13. Tenant screening and background check services

14. Real estate development financing services

15. Real estate project consulting services

16. Real estate sales and marketing automation software

17. Real estate video production and marketing services

18. Real estate financial planning and analysis

19. Property reclamation and redevelopment services

20. Real estate due diligence and risk assessment

21. Real estate investment groups and syndicates

22. Real estate energy efficiency consulting

23. Real estate maintenance and repair services

24. Real estate investment conferences and events

25. Property and casualty insurance for real estate investors

26. Tenant improvement services for commercial real estate

27. Real estate referral services

28. Real estate social media marketing services

29. Real estate accounting and bookkeeping services

30. Real estate investment portfolio analysis

31. Real estate investment and management software

32. Property damage restoration services

33. Tenant retention consulting services

34. Real estate syndication management services

35. Real estate branding and identity design

36. Property tax appeal services

37. Property management accounting software

38. Real estate title and escrow services

39. Real estate valuation software and services

40. Real estate market research and analysis

41. Real estate sales training and coaching

42. Property management staffing and recruitment services

43. Real estate investment and property management analytics

44. Property management payment processing services

45. Real estate market forecasting and trend analysis

46. Real estate investment property inspections

47. Tenant satisfaction survey services

48. Real estate investment tax planning

49. Real estate investment seminars and workshops

50. Real estate litigation and dispute resolution

4. TELECOMMUNICATIONS INDUSTRY

1. Mobile device retail and repair shops

2. Mobile device insurance services

3. Mobile app development services

4. Mobile advertising and marketing agencies

5. Mobile payment processing services

6. Mobile money transfer services

7. Mobile content creation and distribution

8. Mobile network infrastructure and equipment sales

9. Mobile device security software development

10. Mobile device trade-in and upgrade services

11. Mobile broadband services

12. Mobile virtual network operator (MVNO) services

13. Mobile network planning and optimization consulting

14. Mobile device and network testing services

15. Mobile network software development

16. Mobile device rental and leasing services

17. Mobile device recycling and disposal services

18. Mobile device tracking and recovery services

19. Mobile network capacity planning and management

20. Mobile broadband network equipment leasing

21. Mobile   broadband   network   operations   and

maintenance

22. Mobile network engineering and design consulting

23. Mobile network quality of service (QoS) monitoring

24. Mobile device accessory retail and distribution

25. Mobile device and network cybersecurity consulting

26. Mobile device charging station rental and installation

27. Mobile device app store development and management

28. Mobile network spectrum management consulting

29. Mobile network data analytics and reporting

30. Mobile device location-based services (LBS) development and management

31. Mobile device and network performance testing

32. Mobile network planning and design software development

33. Mobile virtual assistant development and management

34. Mobile data center design and construction

35. Mobile device and network supply chain management

36. Mobile network vendor selection and procurement consulting

37. Mobile device and network performance monitoring

38. Mobile device and network forensics consulting

39. Mobile network architecture and topology consulting

40. Mobile device asset tracking and management

41. Mobile device and network configuration management

42. Mobile network software-defined networking (SDN) consulting

43. Mobile device repair and refurbishment services

44. Mobile network customer experience management consulting

45. Mobile network customer care and support services

46. Mobile device and network accessibility consulting

47. Mobile device and network interoperability testing

48. Mobile network billing and revenue management

49. Mobile device and network disaster recovery services

50. Mobile device and network virtualization consulting

4.B. COMMUNICATION INDUSTRY

1. Mobile phone and smartphone manufacturing and distribution services

2. Mobile phone repair and maintenance services

3. Mobile network operator services

4. Fixed-line telecommunications services

5. Internet service provider services

6. Broadband and high-speed internet services

7. Fiber optic and wireless network infrastructure services

8. Cloud communication and data center services

9. Data and network security services

10. Voice over IP (VoIP) and unified communications services

11. Teleconferencing and video collaboration services

12. Virtual private network (VPN) and remote access services

13. Mobile application development and distribution services

14. IT and telecommunications consulting services

15. Web and mobile application hosting and management services

16. Telecommunications and IT project management services

17. Contact center and call center services

18. Telecommunications and IT support and maintenance services

19. Telecommunications and IT infrastructure design and implementation services

20. Telecommunications and IT asset management and procurement services

21. IT and telecommunications training and development

services

22. Telecommunications and IT market research and analysis services

23. IT and telecommunications equipment financing and leasing services

24. IT and telecommunications infrastructure development and financing services

25. Telecommunications and IT performance analysis and benchmarking services

26. IT and telecommunications regulatory compliance and reporting services

27. Telecommunications and IT energy efficiency and sustainability services

28. IT and telecommunications performance management and optimization services

29. Telecommunications and IT system integration and migration services

30. IT and telecommunications data management and analytics services

31. IT and telecommunications workforce management and development services

32. IT and telecommunications market entry and expansion services

33. Mobile payment and financial services technology solutions

34. Social media and digital marketing services

35. E-commerce and online marketplaces

36. Online and mobile advertising services

37. Cybersecurity and digital risk management services

38. Digital identity and authentication services

39. Digital content creation and distribution services

40. Website and online platform design and development services

41. Web and mobile analytics and optimization services

42. Online and mobile reputation management services

43. Digital transformation and strategy consulting services

44. Online and mobile customer engagement and support services

45. Cloud computing and storage services

46. Artificial intelligence and machine learning services

47. Internet of Things (IoT) and smart cities technology solutions

48. Robotics and automation services

49. Big data and analytics services

50. Cybercrime investigation and recovery services

4.C. TECHNOLOGY INDUSTRY

1. Software development and IT services

2. Website design and development services

3. Mobile and app development services

4. Cloud computing and data storage services

5. Cybersecurity and digital risk management services

6. E-commerce and online marketplace services

7. Digital marketing and advertising services

8. Online payment and financial technology services

9. IT consulting and advisory services

10. IT infrastructure and hardware sales and maintenance services

11. IT education and training services

12. IT research and development services

13. IT staffing and human resources management services

14. IT project management and outsourcing services

15. IT support and maintenance services

16. IT security and risk management services

17. IT automation and technology optimization services

18. IT product and software testing services

19. IT product and software licensing and certification

services

20. IT product and software innovation and development services

21. IT product and software marketing and advertising services

22. IT product and software market analysis and strategy services

23. IT product and software pricing strategy and market analysis services

24. IT product and software distribution channel management services

25. IT product and software sales channel optimization services

26. IT product and software sales and marketing training services

27. IT product and software sales and business development services

28. IT product and software supply chain management and optimization services

29. IT product and software labeling and packaging design services

30. IT product and software sustainability and environmentally friendly services

31. IT product and software safety and regulatory compliance services

32. IT product and software traceability and certification services

33. IT product and software traceability and provenance services

34. IT product and software branding and reputation management services

35. IT product and software certification and licensing services

36. IT product and software testing and analysis services

37. IT product and software innovation and product development services

38. IT product and software marketing research and data analysis services

39. IT product and software pricing strategy and market analysis services

40. IT product and software distribution channel management services

41. IT product and software sales channel optimization services

42. IT product and software sales and marketing training services

43. IT product and software sales and business development services

44. IT product and software supply chain management and optimization services

45. IT investment and financial services

46. IT product and software demonstration and field trial services

47. IT product and software promotion and public relations services

48. IT staffing and recruitment services

49. IT product and software customer support and technical assistance services

50. IT product and software brand management and licensing services

5. FINANCE INDUSTRY

1. Commercial banking services
2. Investment banking and securities brokerage services
3. Financial planning and wealth management services
4. Insurance and risk management services
5. Microfinance and small business lending services

6. Consumer lending services

7. Mortgage lending and real estate finance services

8. Asset management and portfolio management services

9. Payment processing and mobile banking services

10. International money transfers and currency exchange services

11. Credit scoring and risk assessment services

12. Financial software and technology solutions

13. Financial consulting and advisory services

14. Financial market research and analysis services

15. Financial education and training services

16. Financial data management and analytics services

17. Crowdfunding and alternative financing platforms

18. Capital markets and securities trading services

19. Corporate finance and restructuring services

20. Financial risk management and insurance services

21. Financial technology innovation and development services

22. Financial security and protection services

23. Financial performance analysis and optimization services

24. Financial data management and compliance services

25. Financial regulatory compliance and audit services

26. Foreign exchange and currency hedging services

27. Financial product and investment design services

28. Financial market entry and expansion services

29. Financial innovation and research services

30. Financial communication and branding services

31. Financial education and literacy services

32. Financial product and service distribution and sales

33. Financial compliance and anti-money laundering services

34. Financial performance benchmarking and analysis services

35. Financial technology integration and implementation services

36. Financial data security and privacy services

37. Financial product and service pricing and profitability analysis

38. Financial marketing and advertising services

39. Financial product and service distribution and logistics services

40. Financial technology and innovation consulting services

41. Financial market risk assessment and management services

42. Financial technology infrastructure and hosting services

43. Financial product and service innovation and design services

44. Financial market entry and competitive analysis services

45. Financial product and service life cycle management services

46. Financial technology and data visualization services

47. Financial product and service customer relationship management services

48. Financial technology and digital transformation services

49. Financial product and service quality control and assurance services

50. Financial product and service user experience design and optimization services

6.A. ENERGY INDUSTRY

1. Solar panel installation and maintenance services

2. Wind turbine installation and maintenance services

3. Geothermal power plant construction and maintenance services

4. Biomass power plant construction and maintenance services

5. Hydroelectric power plant construction and maintenance services

6. Energy efficiency consulting services

7. Energy conservation and management services

8. Energy storage system installation and maintenance services

9. Energy trading and brokerage services

10. Electric vehicle charging station installation and maintenance services

11. Energy project financing and investment services

12. Oil and gas exploration and production services

13. Oil and gas transportation and logistics services

14. Oil and gas refining and processing services

15. Oil and gas storage and distribution services

16. Natural gas liquefaction and transportation services

17. Fuel cell technology development and commercialization

18. Battery technology development and commercialization

19. Power plant construction and maintenance services

20. Power generation equipment manufacturing and distribution

21. Smart grid development and implementation services

22. Energy data analytics and reporting services

23. Renewable energy policy and regulation consulting services

24. Energy project management and construction services

25. Energy asset management and maintenance services

26. Carbon capture and storage (CCS) technology development and commercialization

27. Nuclear power plant construction and maintenance services

28. Mining and extraction of minerals used in energy production (e.g. lithium, cobalt)

29. Fuel distribution and marketing services

30. Renewable energy equipment manufacturing and distribution

31. Energy audit and assessment services

32. Energy education and training services

33. Power plant decommissioning and site remediation services

34. Natural gas storage and distribution services

35. Energy demand response and load management services

36. Waste-to-energy plant construction and maintenance services

37. Electrical and mechanical engineering services for

energy systems

38. Energy forecasting and market research services

39. Energy infrastructure design and planning services

40. Energy-related insurance and risk management services

41. Energy-related legal and regulatory services

42. Environmental impact assessment and mitigation services for energy projects

43. Energy-related public relations and communication services

44. Energy-related market analysis and intelligence services

45. Energy-related software development and analytics services

46. Energy-efficient building design and construction services

47. Energy-efficient appliance manufacturing and distribution

48. Energy-efficient lighting and electrical products manufacturing and distribution

49. Smart thermostat and energy management system manufacturing and distribution

50. Energy-related investment banking and financial advisory services.

6.B. OIL AND GAS INDUSTRY

1. Oil and gas exploration and production

2. Oil and gas drilling and completion services

3. Oil and gas field services and equipment rental

4. Oil and gas transportation and logistics

5. Oil and gas storage and terminal services

6. Oil and gas refining and processing

7. Oil and gas marketing and distribution

8. Oil and gas engineering and consulting services

9. Oil and gas equipment manufacturing and supply

10. Oil and gas software and technology solutions

11. Oil and gas finance and investment services

12. Oil and gas consulting and advisory services

13. Oil and gas legal and regulatory services

14. Oil and gas environmental and sustainability services

15. Oil and gas project management and contracting services

16. Oil and gas human resources and staffing services

17. Oil and gas safety and security services

18. Oil and gas market research and analysis services

19. Oil and gas insurance and risk management services

20. Oil and gas asset management and maintenance services

21. Oil and gas training and professional development services

22. Oil and gas marketing and communications services

23. Oil and gas information technology and data management services

24. Oil and gas renewable energy solutions

25. Oil and gas geotechnical services and drilling support

26. Oil and gas well management and optimization services

27. Oil and gas research and development services

28. Oil and gas data analysis and visualization services

29. Oil and gas automation and control systems

30. Oil and gas power generation and energy management services

31. Oil and gas chemicals and additives manufacturing

32. Oil and gas maintenance and repair services

33. Oil and gas equipment rental and leasing services

34. Oil and gas trade and commerce services

35. Oil and gas recruitment and staffing services

36. Oil and gas exploration and production support services

37. Oil and gas pipeline construction and maintenance services

38. Oil and gas offshore drilling and production services

39. Oil and gas survey and mapping services

40. Oil and gas process improvement and optimization services

41. Oil and gas health, safety, and environmental (HSE) services

42. Oil and gas security and protection services

43. Oil and gas project financing and investment services

44. Oil and gas equipment refurbishment and maintenance services

45. Oil and gas regulatory compliance and audit services

46. Oil and gas renewable energy integration services

47. Oil and gas transportation and storage infrastructure services

48. Oil and gas drilling and completion fluids and additives

49. Oil and gas resource management and optimization services

50. Oil and gas inspection and maintenance services

6. HEALTHCARE INDUSTRY

1. General hospitals

2. Specialist hospitals

3. Diagnostic centers

4. Medical clinics

5. Emergency medical services

6. Rehabilitation centers

7. Mental health clinics

8. Dental clinics

9. Optical clinics

10. Fertility clinics

11. Women's health clinics

12. Pediatric clinics

13. Pharmacy chains

14. Medical equipment rental services

15. Mobile health clinics

16. Health insurance companies

17. Telemedicine services

18. Home healthcare services

19. Medical laboratories

20. Medical transcription services

21. Medical waste disposal services

22. Medical tourism companies

23. Healthcare consulting services

24. Healthcare staffing and recruitment services

25. Elder care services

26. Assisted living facilities

27. Medical supply stores

28. Medical equipment repair and maintenance services

29. Medical research and development companies

30. Nutrition and dietetics services

31. Physiotherapy and rehabilitation services

32. Personalized medicine services

33. Wellness and lifestyle coaching services

34. Hospice and palliative care services

35. Alternative medicine clinics

36. Sports medicine and injury treatment centers

37. Occupational health and safety services

38. Employee health and wellness programs

39. Medical software development companies

40. Healthcare education and training services

41. Healthcare marketing and branding services

42. Clinical research organizations

43. Mobile diagnostic and screening services

44. Healthcare data analytics companies

45. Healthcare product manufacturing

46. Medical content and publishing services

47. Healthcare transportation and logistics services

48. Blood and organ banks

49. Healthcare fundraising and philanthropy services

50. Healthcare technology startups

8. TOURISM INDUSTRY

1. Eco-tourism lodges

2. Luxury hotels

3. Adventure tourism operators

4. Tour operators

5. Travel agencies

6. Car rental services

7. Tourist information centers

8. Guided safari tours

9. Cultural tourism activities

10. Wildlife conservation tours

11. Bird-watching tours

12. Fishing tours

13. Beach resorts

14. Backpacker hostels

15. Boutique hotels

16. Cruise ship operators

17. Theme parks

18. Water parks

19. Amusement parks

20. Historical site tours

21. Mountain trekking tours

22. Scuba diving tours

23. Snorkeling tours

24. Whale watching tours

25. Hiking tours

26. Photography tours

27. Balloon rides

28. River rafting tours

29. Zip lining tours

30. Cultural immersion programs

31. Food and wine tours

32. Music and dance tours

33. Yoga retreats

34. Wellness retreats

35. Language learning programs

36. Volunteer tourism programs

37. Educational tours

38. Religious tourism activities

39. Sport tourism events

40. Golf courses

41. Outdoor adventure equipment rental services

42. Tourist souvenir shops

43. Art galleries

44. Craft markets

45. Local artisan workshops

46. Handicraft cooperatives

47. Traditional dance performances

48. Wildlife rehabilitation centers

49. Botanical gardens

50. Eco-parks

9. FAST-MOVING CONSUMER GOODS (FMCG) INDUSTRY

1. Baked goods production

2. Dairy products production

3. Meat processing

4. Fish processing

5. Snack food production

6. Soft drink manufacturing

7. Juice manufacturing

8. Tea production

9. Coffee production

10. Chocolate and candy production

11. Edible oil manufacturing

12. Spices and seasoning production

13. Baby food production

14. Canned food production

15. Ready-to-eat meals production

16. Breakfast cereal production

17. Packaged pasta production

18. Instant noodle production

19. Flour production

20. Bread and pastry production

21. Frozen food production

22. Bottled water production

23. Alcoholic beverage production

24. Household cleaning products manufacturing

25. Personal care products manufacturing

26. Laundry detergent production

27. Insecticide and pest control products manufacturing

28. Toilet paper and tissue paper production

29. Toothpaste and oral hygiene product manufacturing

30. Soap production

31. Skin care and beauty product manufacturing

32. Hair care product manufacturing

33. Sanitary pad and tampon production

34. Deodorant production

35. Shaving product manufacturing

36. Cosmetics production

37. Pet food production

38. Animal feed production

39. Sugar refining

40. Salt production

41. Dried fruit and nut production

42. Confectionery production

43. Tea and coffee packaging

44. Snack packaging

45. Soft drink packaging

46. Packaged food storage and distribution

47. Paper packaging production

48. Plastic packaging production

49. Glass packaging production

50. Metal packaging production

10. EDUCATION INDUSTRY

1. Online tutoring and coaching services

2. Language training and translation services

3. College admissions consulting and test preparation services

4. STEM education and enrichment programs

5. Early childhood education programs

6. Daycare and after-school care services

7. Corporate training and professional development programs

8. Learning management system (LMS) software development

9. E-learning course development

10. Education consulting and strategic planning services

11. Educational technology (EdTech) product development

12. Academic publishing and textbook production

13. Library and information management services

14. Academic research and consulting services

15. Academic accreditation and evaluation services

16. Educational assessment and testing services

17. Educational supply and equipment sales

18. Educational tours and travel services

19. Educational video production and distribution

20. Educational software development and sales

21. Private school and college operation

22. Language school operation

23. Tutoring and coaching franchise operation

24. Standardized test administration services

25. Student loan and financial aid services

26. Learning disability and special education services

27. Study abroad and cultural exchange services

28. Distance learning and online course providers

29. Educational events and conferences organizing

30. Educational software installation and maintenance services

31. Teacher training and certification programs

32. Vocational training and apprenticeship programs

33. Music and art education programs

34. School supplies and equipment rental services

35. Online learning platform development and management

36. Educational program development for corporate social responsibility initiatives

37. Educational toys and game production and sales

38. Online learning resource marketplace development and operation

39. Student housing and accommodation services

40. Academic writing and editing services

41. College admissions essay consulting services

42. Online college and university course development and delivery

43. Technical and trade school operation

44. Educational app development and sales

45. Learning content management system (LCMS) software development

46. Educational research and development services

47. Continuing education and lifelong learning programs

48. Educational merchandise and souvenir production and sales

49. Educational exhibition and museum operation

50. Educational webinar hosting and promotion

11. TRANSPORTATION INDUSTRY

1. Taxis and private car hire services

2. Commercial trucking and delivery services

3. Cargo and freight logistics services

4. Shipping and maritime transportation services

5. Rail and train transportation services

6. Bus and coach transportation services

7. Logistics and supply chain management services

8. Air transportation and air freight services

9. Fleet management and vehicle maintenance services

10. Urban and public transportation services

11. Heavy machinery and equipment transportation services

12. Vehicle rental and leasing services

13. Road and bridge construction and maintenance services

14. Fuel distribution and management services

15. Maritime security and protection services

16. Warehouse and storage solutions

17. Intermodal transportation and logistics services

18. Transportation infrastructure development and financing services

19. Delivery and courier services

20. Air cargo handling and ground services

21. Rail cargo and freight services

22. Road and bridge toll management services

23. Transportation project management and consulting services

24. Vehicle tracking and telematics services

25. Transportation data management and analysis services

26. Shipping and maritime documentation and clearance services

27. Customs brokerage and trade facilitation services

28. Water transportation and inland waterway services

29. Pipeline transportation and storage services

30. Transportation asset management and leasing services

31. Port and harbor development and management services

32. Transportation safety and regulatory compliance services

33. Heavy equipment rental and leasing services

34. Transportation route optimization and planning services

35. Vehicle parking and management services

36. Intermodal terminal and hub operations services

37. Rail transport engineering and construction services

38. Transportation energy efficiency and sustainability services

39. Shipping and maritime insurance services

40. Urban and public transportation planning and design services

41. Warehouse and distribution center management services

42. Transportation equipment and technology procurement and sourcing services

43. Transportation equipment and technology maintenance and repair services

44. Transportation energy management and optimization services

45. Transportation equipment financing and leasing services

46. Rail and transport project financing and investment services

47. Transportation performance analysis and benchmarking services

48. Shipping and maritime charter services

49. Transportation workforce management and development services

50. Logistics and transportation market entry and expansion services

12. CONSTRUCTION INDUSTRY

1. Residential housing construction
2. Commercial building construction
3. Road construction and maintenance
4. Bridge and overpass construction

5. Dam construction and maintenance

6. Railway construction and maintenance

7. Airport runway and terminal construction

8. Water treatment plant construction

9. Wastewater treatment plant construction

10. Solar power plant construction

11. Wind power plant construction

12. Geothermal power plant construction

13. Hydroelectric power plant construction

14. Gas pipeline construction and maintenance

15. Oil pipeline construction and maintenance

16. Mining infrastructure construction

17. Industrial park construction

18. Sports stadium construction

19. Hospital construction and maintenance

20. University and college construction and maintenance

21. Office building construction

22. Shopping mall construction

23. Public school construction and maintenance

24. Private school construction and maintenance

25. Agricultural infrastructure construction

26. Irrigation system construction and maintenance

27. Landscaping and hardscaping services

28. Environmental remediation and cleanup services

29. Disaster relief and emergency services

30. Demolition and site clearing services

31. Architectural design services

32. Interior design services

33. Building surveying and inspection services

34. Building materials supply and distribution

35. Concrete manufacturing and supply

36. Brick and block manufacturing and supply

37. Steel fabrication and supply

38. Timber and lumber supply

39. Plumbing and electrical services

40. HVAC installation and maintenance

41. Roofing and waterproofing services

42. Painting and finishing services

43. General contracting services

44. Construction equipment rental and leasing

45. Construction management services

46. Green building and sustainability consulting

47. Building automation and smart home technology installation

48. Site security and surveillance services

49. Building maintenance and repair services

50. Specialized niche construction services (e.g., museum exhibit construction, zoo enclosure construction)

12.B. MANUFACTURING INDUSTRY

1. Food and beverage processing

2. Pharmaceuticals and medical supplies manufacturing

3. Textile and clothing manufacturing

4. Furniture and home décor manufacturing

5. Agricultural equipment and machinery manufacturing

6. Building materials and construction supplies manufacturing

7. Electronic and electrical equipment manufacturing

8. Automotive and vehicle parts manufacturing

9. Plastics and polymer manufacturing

10. Chemicals and fertilizers manufacturing

11. Packaging and labeling manufacturing

12. Metal fabrication and machinery manufacturing

13. Cosmetics and personal care product manufacturing

14. Soap and detergent manufacturing

15. Leather and footwear manufacturing

16. Glass and ceramics manufacturing

17. Printing and publishing services

18. Sports and recreational equipment manufacturing

19. Musical instrument manufacturing

20. Toy and game manufacturing

21. Stationery and office supplies manufacturing

22. Household goods and appliances manufacturing

23. Energy and renewable energy products manufacturing

24. Paper and pulp manufacturing

25. Wood products and furniture manufacturing

26. Beauty and wellness product manufacturing

27. Telecommunications and computer hardware manufacturing

28. Industrial machinery and equipment manufacturing

29. Mining and drilling equipment manufacturing

30. Military and defense equipment manufacturing

31. Heavy equipment and earth moving machinery manufacturing

32. Aerospace and aviation parts manufacturing

33. Agricultural chemicals and pesticides manufacturing

34. Landscaping and gardening equipment manufacturing

35. Fitness and sports equipment manufacturing

36. Lighting and electrical equipment manufacturing

37. Plastic bags and packaging manufacturing

38. Adhesives and sealants manufacturing

39. Batteries and energy storage products manufacturing

40. Building materials and supplies manufacturing

41. Medical equipment and supplies manufacturing

42. Office and school supplies manufacturing

43. Home and personal care products manufacturing

44. Consumer goods and electronics manufacturing

45. Machinery and industrial equipment manufacturing

46. Industrial valves and fittings manufacturing

47. Hydraulic and pneumatic components manufacturing

48. Heating and cooling equipment manufacturing

49. Castings and forgings manufacturing

50. CNC machining and precision engineering services

13. SERVICE INDUSTRY

1. Cleaning and janitorial services

2. Home maintenance and repair services

3. Home improvement and remodeling services

4. Home organization and decluttering services

5. Home security and surveillance services

6. Home automation and technology services

7. Personal care and beauty services

8. Personal training and fitness services

9. Personal coaching and counseling services

10. Personal shopping and styling services

11. Personal finance and investment management services

12. Personal transportation and delivery services

13. Personal event planning and coordination services

14. Personal pet care and grooming services

15. Personal photography and videography services

16. Personal tutoring and education services

17. Personal home care and nursing services

18. Personal legal and accounting services

19. Personal concierge and errand services

20. Personal health and wellness services

21. Personal stylist and wardrobe consulting services

22. Personal shopping and retail services

23. Personal event management and event design services

24. Personal travel and tour services

25. Personal digital marketing and advertising services

26. Personal public relations and branding services

27. Personal coaching and mentoring services

28. Personal interior design and decorating services

29. Personal financial planning and wealth management services

30. Personal investment and financial advice services

31. Personal real estate and property management services

32. Personal insurance and risk management services

33. Personal social media and online marketing services

34. Personal writing and content creation services

35. Personal web and graphic design services

36. Personal language and translation services

37. Personal technology and software development services

38. Personal photography and videography services

39. Personal consulting and strategy services

40. Personal project management and outsourcing services

41. Personal catering and food services

42. Personal fashion and beauty services

43. Personal beauty and spa services

44. Personal tutoring and coaching services

45. Personal DJ and entertainment services

46. Personal branding and marketing services

47. Personal marketing research and data analysis services

48. Personal product and brand management services

49. Personal public speaking and presentation services

50. Personal training and certification services

14. STREET BUSINESS (BUYAM SELLEM)

1. Food vending (snacks, fruit, grilled meats)

2. Clothing and apparel (t-shirts, dresses, second-hand clothes)

3. Shoe shining and repair

4. Street-side barbershops

5. Phone charging and repair services

6. Street-side tailors and seamstresses

7. Street-side bike repair shops

8. Food delivery services

9. Mobile money transfer services

10. Street-side car wash services

11. Street-side welding and metal fabrication

12. Street-side furniture makers

13. Flower and plant sales

14. Street-side book and magazine vendors

15. Bicycle rentals and tours

16. Street-side internet cafes

17. Handicrafts and souvenirs

18. Street-side instrument repair shops

19. Street-side photography services

20. Street-side tattoo artists

21. Street-side pet grooming services

22. Street-side plumbing and electrical services

23. Street-side language translation services

24. Street-side key and lock repair shops

25. Street-side car battery charging services

26. Shoe sales and repair

27. Street-side jewelry and accessories

28. Street-side bicycle sales

29. Street-side cooking oil and fuel sales

30. Street-side soap and detergent sales

31. Street-side art sales and exhibitions

32. Street-side fabric and textile sales

33. Street-side butcher shops

34. Street-side seafood vendors

35. Street-side fruit juice and smoothie vendors

36. Street-side coffee and tea vendors

37. Street-side soda and bottled water vendors

38. Street-side ice cream vendors

39. Street-side popcorn and roasted nuts vendors

40. Street-side candy and sweets vendors

41. Street-side breakfast and snack vendors

42. Street-side coconut vendors

43. Street-side roasted maize vendors

44. Street-side plantain and yam vendors

45. Street-side fast food and sandwich vendors

46. Street-side pastry vendors

47. Street-side soup and stew vendors

48. Street-side pizza vendors

49. Street-side falafel and hummus vendors

50. Street-side fresh vegetable and fruit vendors

51. Street-side mobile phone accessory vendors

52. Street-side herbal medicine vendors

53. Street-side hairdressing and hair braiding

54. Street-side car rental services

55. Street-side second-hand electronics sales

56. Street-side beauty and cosmetic sales

57. Street-side bottled gas sales and refills

58. Street-side toy vendors

59. Street-side perfume and fragrance vendors

60. Street-side coconut oil vendors

CONCLUSION

Africa presents numerous opportunities for businesses across a range of industries. However, it is essential to do thorough research and due diligence before investing in any sector or market on the continent, as there are also significant risks and challenges to consider.

DISCLAIMER

The lists provided in the Bishop John's List are not exhaustive and may not be free from errors or omissions. The information provided is intended for general informational purposes only and should not be relied upon as business, financial, or legal advice. Before embarking on any business venture, it is important to conduct thorough research, seek professional guidance, and exercise due diligence to assess the feasibility and potential risks associated with any business endeavor.

Contact Information For those who would like an in-depth guide on investing in Africa, consider buying my book titled "Investing in Africa – A guide to profitable investment opportunities in Africa". You can visit the book page at https://bishopjohn.com. Or you can email us at bishopjohnslist@gmail.com.

Definitions

- **Agritainment**: Agritainment is a term used to describe the combination of agriculture and entertainment, which involves creating an enjoyable experience for visitors while educating them about agriculture and farming practices. It often includes activities such as pick-your-own fruit or vegetable farms, hayrides, corn mazes, pumpkin patches, petting zoos, and other hands-on experiences that give visitors a glimpse into the daily operations of a farm. Agritainment is becoming increasingly popular as a way for farmers to diversify their income streams, attract new customers, and build stronger connections with their local communities.

Sources The lists I provided were compiled based on various sources, including but not limited to:

1. Industry reports and analysis from organizations such as the African Development Bank, the World Bank, and McKinsey & Company

2. Academic literature and research studies on business opportunities in Africa

3. Business publications and websites, such as Forbes Africa and African Business Magazine

4. Online resources and directories for African businesses and entrepreneurs, such as Africa Business Pages and Africa-Trade.ci

5. Interviews and surveys with African business owners, entrepreneurs, and experts in various industries

Please note that the lists are not intended to be comprehensive or definitive, but rather provide a starting point for those interested in exploring potential business opportunities in Africa.

ABOUT THE AUTHOR

About the Author
Bishop John Egyawan

Bishop John Egyawan is a visionary leader, entrepreneur, and advocate for economic empowerment across Africa and the developing world. With a profound understanding of the unique challenges and immense opportunities present in emerging markets, he has dedicated his life to fostering growth, innovation, and sustainable development in these regions.

Born and raised in Ambazonia (Southern Cameroons), Bishop Egyawan's journey is a testament to the power of resilience, hard work, and faith. He has a strong background in Information Technology Management, complemented by various training certificates in the IT field. His academic and professional background, combined with his practical experience, has equipped him with the knowledge and skills to make a tangible impact in various sectors.

As the founder of KaaAfrika by HIM Incorporated, a pioneering water purification and bottling business, Bishop Egyawan has successfully launched and managed multiple ventures across Africa. His company operates in key locations such as Lagos, Nigeria; Ouagadougou, Burkina Faso; Bo, Sierra Leone; and Monrovia, Liberia. Through KaaAfrika, he has not only provided access to high-quality alkaline water but also created jobs and empowered local communities.

Bishop Egyawan's influence extends beyond the business world. As a trained missionary and spiritual leader, he has inspired countless individuals to pursue their dreams and contribute to the betterment of society. His teachings emphasize the importance of faith, integrity, and perseverance in achieving success.

In addition to his entrepreneurial endeavors, Bishop Egyawan is an accomplished author of over ten books including, "The Cross and the sword", "In Their Footsteps" "Holistic Missions", "Holy Manipulation", "Reclaiming Our Destiny", "Eclipsed Sanctity", and "Investing in Africa," provide valuable insights and guidance for those seeking to make a positive impact in developing regions. His latest work, "The Bishop John's List, The Entrepreneur's Blueprint

Cheat Sheet of Over 1400 Profitable Businesses in Africa and the Developing World," combines his extensive knowledge of business with his passion for economic development. This comprehensive guide is a reflection of his commitment to helping entrepreneurs and investors navigate the complex yet rewarding landscape of emerging markets.

Through his books, businesses, and leadership, Bishop John Egyawan continues to inspire a new generation of entrepreneurs to explore and capitalize on the abundant opportunities in Africa and the developing world. His unwavering dedication to economic empowerment and sustainable growth makes him a beacon of hope and a catalyst for change in these regions.

How to Contact the Author.

Email: bishopjohnlist@gmail.com

Phone: +1 301 328 1591

Website: bishopjohn.com

www.ingramcontent.com/pod-product-compliance
Lightning Source LLC
Chambersburg PA
CBHW071947210526
45479CB00002B/843